Responding to domestic abuse

Guidelines for those with pastoral responsibilities

CHURCH HOUSE
PUBLISHING

Church House Publishing
Church House
Great Smith Street
London SW1P 3NZ

ISBN-13 978 0 7151 4108 3
ISBN-10 0 7151 4108 2

GS Misc 838

Printed in England by
Halstan & Co Ltd,
Amersham, Bucks

Published 2006 by Church House Publishing

Copyright © *The Archbishops' Council* 2006

Cover photograph Alison Whitlock
Photography © 2006

Cover design by S2 design and advertising

Tel: 020 7898 1451
Fax: 020 7898 1449

Email: copyright@c-of-e.org.uk

Contents

Contents

Contributors

These guidelines have been developed by a group consisting of the following people:

Kathleen Ben Rabha

Jennifer Beresford

Sue Burridge (Secretary)

Toby Hales

Christopher Jones (Chair)

Ann Memmott

Christine Russell

Jill Sandham

James Woodward

The group were very grateful for the contributions of many others including:

Davina James-Hanman, Margaret Sawyer, Richard Swindell, Ann Fraser and the Southall Black Sisters

Foreword
by the Archbishops of Canterbury and York

In July 2004 the General Synod of the Church of England passed the following motion:

'That this Synod, noting that domestic violence is regarded by the Home Office and the police as a crime:

(a) view with extreme alarm the number of incidents being regularly reported, as being an unacceptable picture of suffering and abuse;

(b) call for national guidelines to be issued by the Archbishops' Council for those with pastoral care responsibilities, as to the appropriate relationship with both victims and perpetrators;

(c) recognise the special circumstances associated with domestic violence, and therefore the special needs of victims, in minority ethnic communities; and

(d) urge all dioceses to consider ways in which they could i) work in partnership with other agencies, co-operating sensitively with those serving minority communities, to provide the resources needed by victims and their families; ii) speak out against the evil of domestic violence; and iii) work for justice and safety in the homes of this nation.

We are delighted to be able to commend these guidelines as one example of the Church's commitment to those who have been victims of domestic abuse and to addressing the processes that lead to domestic abuse. Domestic abuse in all its forms is contrary to the will of God and an affront to human dignity. All need to play their part in preventing or halting it.

We hope that these guidelines will help church communities address the issues in an informed way and be of use to anyone entrusted by victims, survivors or perpetrators to hear their story. In doing so, we acknowledge the excellent work that is already taking place in many churches, by many Christians and by those working in voluntary and statutory organizations and we are grateful for their help in drawing up these guidelines.

✠ Rowan Cantuar:
✠ Sentamu Ebor:

Principles behind the guidelines on domestic abuse[1]

- Belief in God as love expressed in relationships.

- Understanding of humanity (female and male) as made in God's image, and possessing equal worth.

- Equality amongst people and within relationships.

- Refusal to condone any form of abuse.

- Recognition that domestic abuse is prevalent among Christians, as among other groups.

- Acceptance that survivors may choose anyone they trust to talk to, and not necessarily those with pastoral responsibilities.

- Awareness that training for all is essential.

- Partnership with other agencies is the best way to provide informed pastoral care to any child, young person or adult suffering abuse.

- Support, supervision, appraisal and ongoing training for those with pastoral responsibilities is essential.

A working definition of domestic abuse

Any incident of threatening behaviour, violence or abuse **(psychological, physical, sexual, financial or emotional)** between adults who are or have been intimate partners or family members, regardless of gender or sexuality.

(Core Definition agreed by the Governmental Inter-Ministerial group on domestic violence)

NB Although the General Synod motion referred to 'domestic violence', we have chosen to adopt the more wide-ranging term 'domestic abuse' which views violence in a broader context of behaviour over time. Recognizing the sensitivity of terminology, we also decided to use the description 'survivor' for those suffering abuse, except where there were contextual reasons which made the word 'victim' more appropriate.

1. Introduction to the guidelines

1.1   Aims and purposes

As part of a wider motion on domestic abuse (see the Foreword on p. ix) the General Synod called for national guidelines to be issued by the Archbishops' Council for those with pastoral responsibilities. The purposes of these guidelines are:

- to encourage churches to become places of safety for survivors of domestic abuse;

- to identify and outline the appropriate relationship of those with pastoral care responsibilities with both survivors and perpetrators of domestic abuse, including those in minority ethnic communities;

- to provide a brief introduction to the issues;

- to raise awareness about other agencies, support services, resources and expertise, and to encourage collaboration;

- to provide a tool and incentive for further training.

The aim of the guidelines is to inform, direct and equip those working at a local level – not only those working in authorized ministries such as clergy, readers or pastoral assistants, but also those who may be entrusted by survivors or perpetrators to hear their story and who want to offer the most appropriate care. However, these guidelines are, by necessity, brief and are to be seen as an introduction. Excellent resources that cover this subject more thoroughly have been developed by some dioceses, other denominations and agencies, some of which are listed in Section 4.

1.2   Our theological approach

- Authentic Christian theology must proceed from our knowledge of God as love and as One who is known in relationship. This is summed up in the doctrine of the Trinity and the biblical idea of covenant.

- Corresponding to this is our understanding of human beings created in the divine image to live in relationships of love, respect and mutual self-giving. Intimate relationships have the potential to be channels of cherishing and building up.

- Tragically, the corruption of human nature which Christian theology names 'sin' means that the mutual dependence and shared vulnerability which are inseparable from intimacy can instead become the vehicle through which one person can inflict profound hurt and damage upon another.

- The pattern of living that is revealed through Jesus in his relationships with others entails that abuse of any kind is emphatically contrary to the will of God and an affront to human dignity. This entails a heavy responsibility upon the Church and its members to do everything possible to prevent or halt it.

- The good news of Christ promises God's redeeming presence and power in situations of pain and suffering. Through rejection of patterns of violence, and support of those who have been abused, the Church is called to be a vehicle of God's work of healing.

- The Church commends high ideals of love, care and faithfulness in marriage and all intimate relationships. As a body which is present at key moments when relationships are blessed publicly, it has a responsibility to offer authentic teaching and appropriate pastoral care.

- It is therefore particularly disturbing that not only has the Church failed at many points to protect the vulnerable and to address the processes that lead to domestic abuse, but has also (intentionally or unintentionally) reinforced abuse, failed to challenge abusers and intensified the suffering of survivors.

- Detailed examination reveals that this is a failure not only in practice but also in the assumptions and beliefs which inform practice. The Church has not always done justice to the truth about God and human beings that is revealed in the Christian Gospel, and its teaching has often contained sub-Christian elements which have distorted or denied that life-giving truth.

- We are conscious of the obligation of Christian theology to listen to the testimony of those who suffer in particular ways, and have sought throughout to give full weight to the perspectives and needs of those who have been subject to domestic abuse.

- The appendix on 'harmful theology' seeks to outline how wrong or misguided forms of Christian belief may aggravate the sufferings of those who are abused and stand in the way of effective preventative and remedial action. It also suggests how healthy and sensitive teaching in the Church may avoid these pitfalls and make a positive contribution to countering abuse.

1.3   Context

In 2002 the Methodist Conference received research into domestic abuse in the Methodist Church. The findings included evidence that its incidence in the Methodist Church reflected the incidence in society as a whole. It is unlikely that this would be different for the Church of England, yet until recently domestic abuse was rarely discussed in Church communities. In 2005 the Methodist Conference received a comprehensive report called *Taking Action: Domestic Abuse and the Methodist Church*, which we commend for further reading (see Section 4). We also commend the excellent work done by some dioceses in trying to raise the profile of the issues and provide resources and training. We recognize too the expertise and valuable ministry of many Christians working with both survivors and perpetrators in voluntary and statutory organizations.

There is growing awareness in society of the extent of domestic abuse and recognition that domestic abuse is a crime, not a private matter to be kept in the family or community. This has resulted in changed legislation and a planned programme of interventions by police, housing and other statutory or voluntary agencies designed to improve safety, encourage partnership working and provide more support for survivors. Many of these agencies have been extremely supportive of the development of these guidelines and are keen to work with the Church to support survivors and reduce the incidence of domestic abuse.

For the Church, support of survivors and response to perpetrators of domestic abuse must be considered in the wider context of good pastoral care. These guidelines should be considered in conjunction with *Protecting all God's children: The Child Protection Policy for the Church of England* and the guidelines for protecting vulnerable adults, *Promoting a safe church*.

1.4 How to use this document

In preparing this resource, we have recognized that people will approach it with different needs and expectations, depending on their circumstances. Those dealing with an urgent or novel pastoral situation will rightly look for clear, concise and accessible practical guidance. This we seek to provide in Section 3.1 *Guidelines for those with pastoral responsibility* (pp. 10–12) in the form of bullet points beginning 'Do' or 'Do not'. These constitute basic rules to be observed for the sake of safety and good practice.

Part of the purpose of issuing guidelines is that the Church of England should adopt policies for action at both parish and diocesan level. We therefore offer 3.2 *Guidelines for a parish* (pp. 12–13) and 3.3 *Guidelines for a diocese* (pp. 13–14) as examples of good practice. These are somewhat less specific than the 'front-line' pastoral guidelines, but are no less important, because they aim to build good practice, training and review of this area into the continuing life of the institution. They are not exhaustive, but we believe that to implement them will initiate a process of raising awareness and learning from experience which will deepen the Church's engagement with the task of care and protection.

Understanding policy and practice requires background information. We therefore preface the guidelines with a summary of our theological approach (Section 1.2, pp. 1–2), an explanation of the context in which the guidelines have been produced (Section 1.3, pp. 2–3), some basic facts about domestic abuse (Section 2, pp. 4–5) and the helpful disclosure flow chart (p. 9), taken with permission from the Methodist Church's good practice guidelines. We follow the guidelines with a note on Where to go next (p. 15), which in most cases will be to local organizations, and a short list of basic Resources (p. 16).

Beyond this, we found a number of topics which called for more extended comment and reflection. They range from information about the law and the needs of particular groups (children, survivors, women in minority ethnic communities, older people and perpetrators), through vivid accounts of the experience of survivors, to consideration of specific areas in which the Church needs to examine its ways of working (theology, marriage preparation and clergy discipline). Since it would have been unwieldy and confusing to include this material in the guidelines, the topics have been dealt with in a series of appendices (pp. 17–52), which can be consulted as needed.

2. Domestic abuse: the facts

In building on the working definition, it must be emphasized that in the overwhelming majority of cases domestic abuse is found to be a pattern of repeated behaviour rather than an isolated incident.

2.1   Facts about domestic abuse

- Domestic abuse affects 1 in 5 adults in this country at some point in their lives (1 in 4 women and 1 in 7 men).

- One-quarter of all assaults reported to the police are defined as domestic abuse.

- An average of 2 women a week are killed by their male partner or ex-partner in England and Wales.[2]

- In 2004–2005 45 per cent of female homicide victims were killed by their present or former partner.[3]

- 1 in 3 suicide attempts is by a victim of domestic abuse.[4]

- Domestic abuse costs the UK approximately £23 billion a year in direct and indirect costs.[5]

- Every minute police receive a call about domestic abuse.[6]

- On one day in 2000, of all the domestic abuse calls received by the police, 81 per cent were women attacked by men; 8 per cent were men attacked by women; 7 per cent were men attacked by men; 4 per cent were women attacked by women.[7]

- On average there will have been 35 assaults before a victim calls the police.[8]

- Up to 5 per cent of older people in the community suffer from verbal abuse and up to 25 per cent are the victims of physical or financial abuse.[9]

- All domestic abuse is a fundamental violation of human rights, and much of it is criminal.

- Domestic abuse occurs in all types of households and amongst all professions, including clergy and those in positions of leadership.

Facts about the effects on children

- At least 750,000 children a year witness domestic abuse.[10]

- 33 per cent of these had seen their mother beaten severely and 10 per cent had witnessed sexual abuse.[11]

- The Department of Health states that 75 per cent of children on the Child Protection Register are living with domestic abuse in the home.[12]

- 29 children were killed by a parent during parental contact disputes involving an abusive partner in the period from 1994 to 2004.[13]

2.2   What is domestic abuse?

All forms of abuse cause damage to the survivor, particularly to their self-esteem, and express an imbalance of power in the relationship. Abuse can on rare occasions happen once, but usually it is a systematic, repeated and often escalating pattern of behaviour by which the abuser seeks to control, limit and humiliate,[14] often behind closed doors.

Abusive behaviour can take many forms and the following examples are not exhaustive.

Physical

For example, hitting; slapping; burning; pushing; restraining; giving too much medication or the wrong medication; assault with everyday implements such as kitchen knives; kicking; biting; punching; shoving; smashing someone's possessions; imprisoning them; or forcing them to use illegal drugs as a way of blackmailing and controlling them.

Psychological

For example, shouting; swearing; frightening; blaming; ignoring or humiliating someone; blackmailing them; threatening harm to children or pets if they misbehave; ridiculing every aspect of their appearance and skills; keeping them deliberately short of sleep; being obsessively and irrationally jealous; keeping them isolated from friends and family; threatening suicide or self-harm.

Financial

For example, the illegal or unauthorized use of someone's property, money, pension book or other valuables; forcing them to take out loans; keeping them in poverty; demanding to know every penny they spend; refusing to let them use transport or have money to pay for it.

Sexual

For example, forcing someone to take part in any sexual activity without consent, e.g. rape or sexual assault; forcing them or blackmailing them into sexual acts with other people; forcing children to watch sexual acts; sexual name-calling; imposition of dress codes upon a partner; involvement in the sex trade or pornography; knowingly passing on Sexually Transmitted Infections; controlling access to contraception.

Spiritual

For example, telling someone that God hates them; refusing to let them worship (e.g. not allowing a partner to go to church); using faith as a weapon to control and terrorize them for the abuser's personal pleasure or gain; using religious teaching to justify abuse (e.g. 'submit to your husband'), or to compel forgiveness.

Neglect

For example, depriving someone of food, shelter, heat, clothing, comfort, essential medication or access to medical care.

2.3   Who experiences domestic abuse?

People experience domestic abuse regardless of their social group, class, ethnicity, age, disability or sexuality. Most abuse is carried out by men against female partners, but abuse can be inflicted by women on men, and can also occur in same-sex relationships. There is also evidence of parents being abused by teenage children and of the elderly being abused by members of their family. Domestic abuse occurs among people within our church communities. Clergy and prominent members of churches have been found to be abusers.[15]

Domestic abuse is a gender-biased phenomenon: the incidents of abuse of women are very much more frequent and more severe. Women are more likely to worry about not having money or anywhere to live. Women with children who are being abused may fear that the children will be taken away from them if they speak out (see Appendix 4).

If the victim is a partner of a member of the clergy the issues of disclosure are problematic because their relationship is particularly public and usually their home comes with the clergyperson's job (see Appendix 10).

It is important not to generalize about people from black and minority ethnic backgrounds. As in any community, there are huge variations in education, sophistication and development. It is critical not to assume that values held in 'British' culture are always progressive and at odds with those of minority communities. Nevertheless it is important that 'honour' crimes, forced marriage and female genital mutilation are recognized by the Home Office and the police as forms of domestic abuse.

Domestic violence exists in all races, classes, cultures and religions. It is a widespread and hidden problem in all communities. But the rates of reporting vary between different communities. There is little or no nationwide data on the extent of domestic violence within minority communities. What is clear, however, is that domestic violence is grossly under-reported in these communities for a variety of reasons.

In minority communities, cultural and religious traditions can have a particular stranglehold on women and children who wish to exercise their right to live free from violence and abuse, as can racism in the wider society and state policies such as the operation of immigration and asylum laws and rules. The experiences of black and minority women are often invisible because they do not fit neatly into categories of race or gender. Instead they face multiple forms of discrimination, which is only just beginning to be acknowledged (see Appendix 6).

Children in the family are also victims of domestic abuse, directly and indirectly. Section 120 of the Children and Adoption Act 2002 defines 'harm' to include 'impairment from seeing or hearing the ill-treatment of another'. Being a victim or witness of domestic abuse can have a severe effect on a child's behaviour, health or educational performance in ways that are likely to be visible at Sunday school or in the youth group and can create long-term relational problems. These can include low self-esteem, withdrawal or anxiety, and behavioural problems. Conversely, children may be overly anxious to please and unnaturally well-behaved. This response may be less obvious and frequently meets with adult approval rather than concern. Children are often more aware of the abuse than their parents realize (see Appendix 4).[16]

The 2001 British Crime Survey suggests that male victims are half as likely to report as female victims. Feelings of shame and embarrassment may preclude a male partner from disclosing abuse to anyone. As with female victims, the threats of losing all or most contact with the children can be a major hold on a male victim, keeping them tied to an abusive partner. Trying to ward off an attack could be interpreted by an abusive female partner, police or courts as a violent attack. Some male victims report facing arrest because the police tend to assume that the woman is the victim.

2.4   Who perpetrates domestic abuse?

As has been stated above (p. 6), the vast predominance of domestic abuse is inflicted by men upon women. The dynamics of women-upon-men and same-sex abuse appear to be significantly different. Abuse by men towards women appears to reflect expectations of exercising power and control over the partner – what is sometimes referred to as a sense of 'entitlement'. It is a deliberate choice for which the abuser must be held responsible, and it is supported by the abuser's belief either that the behaviour is defensible or that he is not to blame for it.

Perpetrators come from all walks of life and professions. The behaviour they exhibit in public can be very different from their private behaviour to their partners. Often the abusive partner is able to be charming in public yet switch to abusive conduct quickly when behind closed doors and alone with the partner. The abuser can also exhibit rapid changes in behaviour, being loving and apologetic towards the partner at one moment and abusive the next. They often will not hesitate to say sorry and to say it will never happen again. For long periods the situation may appear tolerable. However, experience shows that abuse will almost invariably happen again and will get worse.

Triggers of abusive or violent behaviour appear to include cohabitation, marriage, pregnancy, infidelity by the partner or the threat to leave, each of which may contribute in different ways to the misplaced sense of 'entitlement'. However, abuse can take place without any particular external causes and often becomes routine. The operation of these patterns of intimidation, self-justification and deception means that the behaviour of perpetrators is not easy to counter. The abuser generally relies upon the difficulty and the stigma of reporting abuse to deter the victim from taking effective action and may threaten further violence or damage to the victim's reputation in the event of disclosure.

Most practical work in the area of domestic abuse has understandably focused on providing safety and support to survivors. Action to change the behaviour of perpetrators is difficult to initiate and problematic to evaluate, but since the 1990s increasing attention has been given to 'perpetrator programmes'. It is rightly said that the primary aim of working with perpetrators remains the protection of women and children, with the secondary aim of holding perpetrators to account and promoting respectful relationships,[17] but the evidence for the effectiveness of such programmes remains inconclusive and controversial (see Appendix 9).

It is vital that church workers should not attempt work with perpetrators which is inappropriate or for which they are not qualified. For reflections on realistic responses, see Appendix 9.

According to Action on Elder Abuse, the greatest number of calls concerning the elderly in their homes identify the abuser as a family member who does not have direct responsibility for the victim's care (see Appendix 7).[18]

A disclosure flow chart

Taken with permission from the Methodist Good Practice guidelines

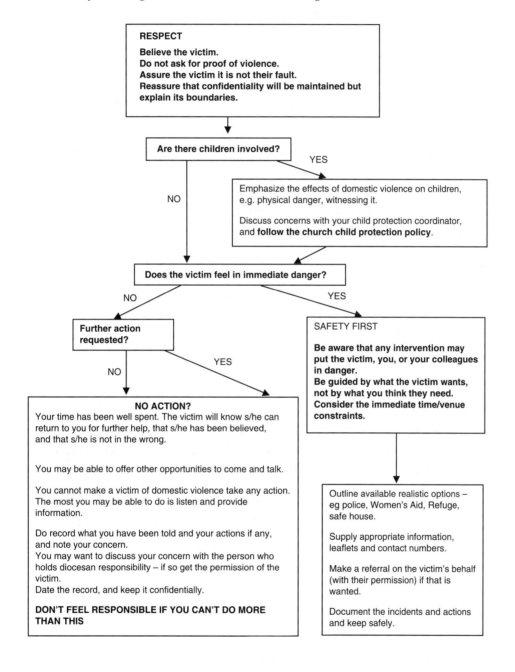

RESPECT

Believe the victim.
Do not ask for proof of violence.
Assure the victim it is not their fault.
Reassure that confidentiality will be maintained but explain its boundaries.

Are there children involved?

YES

NO

Emphasize the effects of domestic violence on children, e.g. physical danger, witnessing it.

Discuss concerns with your child protection coordinator, and **follow the church child protection policy.**

Does the victim feel in immediate danger?

NO

YES

Further action requested?

NO

YES

SAFETY FIRST

Be aware that any intervention may put the victim, you, or your colleagues in danger.
Be guided by what the victim wants, not by what you think they need.
Consider the immediate time/venue constraints.

NO ACTION?
Your time has been well spent. The victim will know s/he can return to you for further help, that s/he has been believed, and that s/he is not in the wrong.

You may be able to offer other opportunities to come and talk.

You cannot make a victim of domestic violence take any action. The most you may be able to do is listen and provide information.

Do record what you have been told and your actions if any, and note your concern.
You may want to discuss your concern with the person who holds diocesan responsibility – if so get the permission of the victim.
Date the record, and keep it confidentially.

DON'T FEEL RESPONSIBLE IF YOU CAN'T DO MORE THAN THIS

Outline available realistic options – eg police, Women's Aid, Refuge, safe house.

Supply appropriate information, leaflets and contact numbers.

Make a referral on the victim's behalf (with their permission) if that is wanted.

Document the incidents and actions and keep safely.

3. The guidelines

3.1 Guidelines for those with pastoral responsibility

What to be aware of

Those suffering abuse are likely to turn to someone they trust, who may or may not be in a position of responsibility. However, if you are concerned that someone you know might be a victim, you may notice that she/he exhibits one of more of the following behaviours:

- has unexplained bruises or injuries;

- shows signs of feeling suicidal;

- becomes unusually quiet or withdrawn;

- has panic attacks;

- has frequent absences from work or other commitments;

- wears clothes that conceal even on warm days;

- stops talking about her/his partner;

- is anxious about being out or rushes away.

How to help

- Most survivors want to be asked. If you are able to broach the subject, your offer of help could be the first step in enabling them to seek help; e.g. 'How are things at home?' and if it becomes appropriate, 'Is anyone hurting you?'

- Do try wherever possible to talk in a safe, private place where you will not be interrupted, or arrange to talk again (but someone in distress may start talking anywhere).

- Do try to make it clear that complete confidentiality cannot be guaranteed, depending on the nature of what is disclosed.

- Do dial 999 if you are witnessing a violent incident or if the person needs medical care.

- Do take plenty of time to listen and believe what they say. If they sense disbelief they may be discouraged from speaking again.

- Do be sensitive to people's backgrounds and cultures and check your own and their understanding of how the cultural issues affect them. Ask them about the attitude of their families and what support they can expect.

- Do affirm the strength and courage it takes to have survived the abuse and even more to talk about it.

- Do express concern for their safety and discuss it. Do they have somewhere to stay?

- Do ask about the children. Are they abused or witnesses to abuse? If so you may need to persuade them to report it or allow you to do so. You may have no option but to do so if a child is at risk (see Appendix 4).

- Do encourage them to focus on their own needs, something they may not have been able to do since the abuse began but which is critical in helping them to change their situation.

- Do reassure them that, whatever the circumstances, abuse is not justified and not their fault.

- Do ask them what they want from you and the parish. Offer help which is in response to their needs and preferences and which lets them keep in control.

- Do check if it is all right to contact them at home before doing so.

- Do keep information confidential and never pass on an address without consent (unless it is a child protection issue).

- Do give information about where to get specialist help (see Section 4), particularly help that is available locally. Do encourage them to seek professional help even if they do not want to leave.

- Do make a brief objective note of date, facts and context of what you have been told but keep your opinions separate. This should be kept in strict confidence but could be useful in any future prosecution (see Appendix 3).

- Do not trivialize, judge, criticize or dismiss what they tell you.

- Do not have physical contact.

- Do not put yourself in a dangerous position. Do not confront the alleged abuser or offer to mediate.

- Do not give advice, suggest they 'try again' or make decisions for them or try to take control. Discuss their options, find out what *they* want (bearing in mind that sometimes their wishes will have been manipulated by the perpetrator) and help them to achieve it. They may change their mind several times. You may experience feelings of frustration, but the choice has to be theirs otherwise you are mirroring the behaviour of an abuser.

- Do not expect them to make decisions in a hurry. Leaving may be as frightening as staying. Helping them build a contingency/crisis plan can make them feel in control of their life.

- Do not forget your own needs. Such disclosures will be stressful for you. Discuss the situation with a specialist or supervisor without identifying the victim.

The following points are of particular relevance when dealing with survivors from a minority ethnic background[19]

- Do remember that the need to build a sense of security and trust, which applies to all encounters with survivors, is likely to be intensified for those from minority ethnic communities.

- Do take extreme care before deciding whether family or community support networks would be beneficial – they might be part of the problem.

- Do make referrals, as far as possible, for support and advice to organizations from the same background as the survivor, with a reliable track record of helping survivors.

- Do make referrals to specialist practitioners and organizations if immigration or asylum issues are involved.

- Do make an accurate record of allegations of domestic abuse, since this may be vital in enabling someone with insecure immigration status to obtain indefinite leave to remain in the UK.

- Do consider what financial and other support can be offered to a survivor whose immigration status is insecure and who cannot access housing or benefits.

- Do make sure that any interpreter speaks the correct language, and dialect, and that the survivor feels comfortable with this person (issues of confidentiality may arise if the interpreter is from the same community).

- Do continue to provide befriending and support, remembering the isolation, shame and poverty which may befall women from minority communities whose marriages break up.

- Do not attempt to mediate or reconcile out of respect for cultural difference. This places the survivor at further risk of abuse.

- Do not allow lack of secure immigration or asylum status to prevent attempts to ensure the safety of the survivor.

- Do not use children as interpreters, since they may have experienced or witnessed violence and been deeply affected by it.

3.2   Guidelines for a parish

- A parish that takes domestic abuse seriously should discuss the issue with the PCC and decide on realistically achievable action.

- When raising awareness of this issue remember that it is very probable that someone in the PCC has personal experience of abuse, so it may arouse deep emotions and stir up memories. Within any given year, 1 woman in 9 is currently experiencing domestic abuse; this suggests at least 1 man in 9 is perpetrating abuse. Others will have family members or close friends who are being abused, still others will have experienced it in the home when they were children or young people.

- Display posters, leaflets and local information about where help is available, and keep this up to date. Literature and information should reflect different ethnic perspectives and promote cultural sensitivity in appropriate ways.

- Invite a speaker from the police, Women's Aid or a recognized agency (see Where to go next, p. 15) to talk to all members of the church community. Anyone could be taken into confidence by someone suffering abuse, so it is important that everyone knows about the subject.

- Include in marriage preparation themes of equality, entitlement, conflict, violence and control (see Appendix 8).

- Ensure that programmes for children and young people include appropriate opportunities to talk about dealing with anger and violence. Those children who have lived with violence want to talk about it and make sense of their experiences. Young people often find it easier to talk to peers than adults,[20] so create opportunities for paired and small group work. Offer support to confidants.

- Give financial support to one of your local projects or an organization (see Where to go next).

- Consider what support can be given to survivors from minority ethnic backgrounds and those with insecure immigration status, and to organizations working with them.

- Organize courses in parenting and confidence-building skills.

- Challenge inappropriate comments or behaviour by church members.

- Encourage leaders and those who preach to speak out against domestic abuse in teaching, sermons, prayers and parish magazines – bearing in mind that many of the congregation may have personal experiences.

3.3   Guidelines for a diocese

- A diocese that takes domestic abuse seriously should consider appointing a named person, or group of people, who will undertake further training and act as a resource for the diocese.

- Circulate among clergy, lay leaders, Mothers' Unions and PCCs guidelines on helping victims of abuse with a local directory of sources of help. This information should be available in every church and updated regularly. It is readily available from your local Domestic Violence Forum or local council (see Resources on p. 16).

- Offer training days in the CME programme for parish clergy, archdeacons, the bishop's visitor and lay people, involving the police, Women's Aid and local groups who are active members of the local domestic violence partnerships. Include some awareness of cultural differences and all kinds of abuse.

- Make sure you have a clear complaints procedure, take allegations against clergy and church workers very seriously, and take steps to inform the police. Consider the correlation with child abuse. Domestic abuse is usually a repeated pattern that continues in spite of the apparent remorse of the abuser.

- Aim to provide for all clergy to receive support, supervision, appraisal and ongoing training as a mandatory feature of their ministry, and ensure that there are people trained in supervision to provide it.

- Consider collaborative projects aimed at promoting guidelines and training in partnership with other denominations and faith communities.

- Ensure that new clergy and their spouses have support or know where it is available when they move to the diocese.

Where to go next

The most useful resources are ones available locally. Find out about such resources by contacting your local Domestic Violence Forum (http://www.womensaid.org.uk) or the community safety/crime reduction unit of your local council. Local authorities now have assessment targets for domestic abuse, which includes producing a directory of local services updated at least every two years. You should be able to have copies of these to give to people.

Free legal advice for victims of domestic abuse may be available from:

Women's Aid, Refuge, Rights of Women or MALE.

Most police forces now have either a specialist domestic violence unit or domestic violence coordinators who are experienced in dealing with these cases and can offer training. Find out the name of your local officer.

We have not included a long list of organizations because of the need to keep up to date. The BBC web site http://www.bbc.co.uk/health/hh/links.shtml has a selection of organizations selected by experts in the field and which is strictly monitored.

4. Resources for training and raising awareness

A selection of church resources:

Jennifer Beresford, *Creating Confidence in Women*, SPCK, 1998.

Breaking the Silence on Domestic Violence: a domestic violence leaflet produced by Church in Society, Robert Runcie House, 2–3 Bedford Place, Maidstone, Kent, ME16 8JB.

Domestic Abuse and the Methodist Church: Taking Action, Methodist Publishing House, 2005. Includes theology, prayer cards and draft good practice. Tel. 01733 325002.

Enduring the Silence CD-ROM resource pack produced by Diocese of Chester, Church House, Lower Lane, Aldford, Chester, CH3 6HP.

Out of the Shadows: Steps towards ending violence – a community-based approach: a Mothers' Union resource pack for use by trained facilitators for work with groups on violence including domestic abuse. http://www.themothersunion.org

Shattered Love . . . Broken Lives . . .: a domestic violence resource pack and CD from the Domestic Violence Task Group of Churches Together in the Merseyside Region. Tel. 0151 709 0125.

'What is this place?', Churches Together in England, 2004. Six studies that follow the journey a woman experiencing violence may make, from recognition of her situation to making a new beginning. Available from: Edith Steele, Churches Together in England, 27 Tavistock Square, London, WC1H 9HH. Tel. 020 7529 8132. Email: Edith.Steele@CTE.org.uk

Broken Rites

An association of divorced and separated wives of clergy, ministers and Church Army Officers living in England, Wales, Scotland, Northern Ireland and the Republic of Ireland. http://www.brokenrites.org

Harmful theology

As stated in Section 1.2 above, the purpose of this Appendix is to draw attention to misguided or distorted versions of Christian belief which have contributed to the problem of domestic abuse, and by contrast to highlight 'life-giving' theology which may help the Church to counter abuse and encourage healthy relationships.

A1.1   Introduction

Christians see a strong affinity between the character of God and the way of life to which God's people are called. We believe that God creates us in the divine image to express his life-giving love in our actions and relationships. The beliefs about God that occupy the mind and imagination of members of the Church can be expected both to reflect and to shape their conduct towards others.

It has also been said that 'God created human beings in his own image and they returned the compliment.' It is inevitable, and generally helpful, that our understanding of God should draw upon associations and analogies from our experience of human relationships. This enables our everyday life to illuminate our experience of God, but also to be corrected by our knowledge of God as the creator and perfecter of what is good in this world.

However, it carries the danger that our perception of God may be distorted and that this perception may in turn reinforce inappropriate or even pathological patterns of behaviour. Over the centuries questionable assumptions about the relation between men and women, which were supposed to reflect the will of God, have influenced the Church's interpretation of the Bible, its moral teaching and pastoral practice. Through increasing awareness of the damaging effects of these elements in the tradition, the Churches have begun to reassess and critically revise parts of their theological inheritance.

Domestic abuse is not simply an isolated series of events between a perpetrator and a victim but reflects the wider factors influencing their relationship. It is a tragic fact that bad theology, in this case a faulty understanding of God and human beings in relationship, can have the effect – whether intended or not – of betraying victims of domestic abuse and encouraging the actions of perpetrators.

A1.2   God the abuser?

Domestic abuse is fundamentally an abuse of power, and many conceptions of God derived from the Bible and the Christian tradition have portrayed divine power in unhealthy and potentially oppressive ways. There are particular problems in the attribution of violent actions and attitudes to God, chiefly but not solely in the Old Testament, which require careful interpretation with reference to the historical and theological context.

Even short of this, the divine–human relationship may be conceived in terms of domination and submission at the expense of grace, mercy and patient love. When used as a model for human relationships, this emphasizes authority and obedience at the expense of mutuality. In combination with uncritical use of masculine imagery to characterize God, it can validate overbearing and ultimately violent patterns of behaviour in intimate relationships. The 'post-Christian' feminist Mary Daly had a point – despite the crudity of its formulation – when she said in the 1970s, 'If God is male, then the male is God.'

Church teaching and preaching must correct this major imbalance by holding fast to the ministry, death and resurrection of Jesus Christ as the decisive revelation of the divine character. This makes it clear that (in the words of a traditional Anglican collect) God 'declares his almighty power chiefly in showing mercy and pity'.

The ministry of Jesus shows respect and compassion for women, children and vulnerable people, expressing the power of God counter-culturally in healing and restoration. The death of Jesus shows that God identifies with the victims rather than the perpetrators of violence. In contrast to some theologies which seem to attribute redemptive power to violence, in terms either of sacrifice or punishment, Jesus neither compromises with violence nor denies its destructive effects. The resurrection of Jesus confirms that the path of love and endurance is the way blessed by God, and the powers of sin and death will not finally prevail against it.

This central paradigm emphasizes that God, far from being an abuser, is the guardian of the oppressed, the victor over violence and the source of love, healing and hope. In interpreting the diverse material and varying perspectives of the Bible, we need to ensure that our controlling vision is determined by what God has made known through Jesus and that our beliefs are tested by their moral and practical fruits.

A1.3   Human relationships – between good and evil

Domestic abuse must also be set against the background of what people believe about human relationships and potential. A Christian understanding of human nature embraces both the good and the evil of which human beings are capable, pointing to the ways in which we may hurt and degrade one another but also to the possibility of transformation.

This understanding needs careful specification in relation to domestic abuse. Idealized doctrines of marriage and love have often blinded Christians to the reality of manipulative and violent behaviour – overwhelmingly on the part of men. The emerging social consensus that domestic abuse is not to be tolerated must be accompanied by a church consensus that it is an offence against God and against people created in his image.

For the perpetrator it is a manifestation of the illusory desire to be 'like God' in seeking to dominate and avoid being held accountable for one's actions – though ironically this is the reverse of the character of God made known in Christ. Philippians 2.5–11 celebrates the coming of Jesus in the form of a servant, showing that true likeness to God is found not in selfish grasping but in humble self-giving.

If this is true, it follows that the application in the New Testament (Ephesians 5.25–33) of the model of Christ and the Church to the relation between husband and wife has the effect of subverting false ideas of authority and power. The 'authority' of the man consists in authorization to give himself in love to his wife: 'husbands should love their wives as they do their own bodies' (Ephesians 5.28).

Following the pattern of Christ means that patterns of domination and submission are being transformed in the mutuality of love, faithful care and sharing of burdens. 'Be subject to one another out of reverence for Christ' (Ephesians 5.21). Although strong patriarchal tendencies have persisted in Christianity, the example of Christ carries the seeds of their displacement by a more symmetrical and respectful model of male–female relations.

A1.4   Sin and responsibility

Theology must take account of the insight from developmental psychology that all human relationships are conditioned by domestic experiences. Learned behaviour and attitudes within the family unit have effects, for good and ill, upon subsequent relationships.

Marriage and other intimate relationships have potential for healing: in the emotional affirmation and support which couples offer to one another, the psychological hurts sustained in earlier life can be contained and overcome. Conversely, those hurts may contribute to the failure of relationships and as a result may be reinforced and deepened.

In Christian understanding sin includes both what we do and what is done to us through the relationships and systems in which we live. A realistic view must recognize both that human beings act under the impact of negative influences and temptations, and that they have some degree of control (depending on circumstances) over what they do. Sometimes people choose evil and even find fulfilment in it.

Responsibility for domestic abuse is not mitigated by the factors that condition the behaviour of perpetrators. However, the destructive dynamics of sin must be taken into account when thinking about the possibility of change. Because of the traumatic and life-threatening effects of domestic abuse, sober realism about the behaviour of perpetrators is necessary. Despite his compassion and hopefulness, Jesus reserved strong words of condemnation for the abusers of children (Matthew 18.6) and the Churches must not compromise in their identification of domestic abuse as sin.

A1.5   The abuse of humility

While theologies of domination have had a pernicious effect in encouraging abusive behaviour by men, the corrective, a theology of humility, has often been misapplied to women, increasing the imbalance between the expectations of each sex held by churches and societies. It has been forgotten that Jesus' teaching and ministry not only humbled the exalted but exalted the humble.

Perversely, the example of Christ's sacrificial self-giving has been applied disproportionately to those who need affirmation and encouragement rather than negation and criticism, and particularly to women in situations of subordination and dependence. It has encouraged compliant and passive responses by women suffering in abusive relationships.

In many traditions the portrayal of the Virgin Mary as the archetypal woman has often functioned to reinforce norms of female passivity and obedience to men, to restrict the social role of women to the bearing and nurturing of children, and to contrast the affirmation of female sexuality unfavourably with the ideal of virginal purity. However, a careful interpretation of the narratives about Mary in the New Testament places her humility and obedience towards God in the context of free consent, active discipleship and visionary faith in the coming of God's kingdom. Her song of praise, the Magnificat (Luke 1.46–55) celebrates the toppling of the powerful from their thrones and the lifting up of the lowly – hardly an uncritical submission to patriarchal oppression.

Most seriously, the theology of self-denial and redemptive suffering which flows from the crucifixion of Jesus and the symbol of the cross has often undermined people's recognition of the evils being done to them and implanted masochistic attitudes of acceptance, or even celebration, of their afflictions.

This is a complex problem, which requires discernment in particular cases, but there are major objections to comparing the suffering resulting from domestic abuse with the suffering of Jesus and Christian disciples or martyrs.

First, there is the *purpose* of such suffering. Jesus and the martyrs accepted a vocation to suffer as a consequence of bearing witness to the love, truth and justice of God. Although survivors are sometimes urged to persist in abusive relationships in order to change the attitude of the perpetrator, it is not convincing to find redemptive value in passive acceptance of abuse and violence.

Second – and related – there is an element of *freedom*, of positive deliberation and decision, in the action of Jesus and the martyrs. However, in the acceptance of abuse and the continuance of oppression there is no true freedom on the part of the victim.

If the divine purpose embodied in Jesus is to bring 'life in all its fullness' (John 10.10), it is impossible to see domestic abuse as a means of fulfilling it. The Church needs to make a clear distinction between submission to abuse and genuine self-denial, which is a gateway to abundant life and a means of bringing good out of evil.

A1.6   Forgiveness, repentance and justice

Harmful theology affects the response of churches when domestic abuse comes to light or reaches a critical point. A spirituality of self-denial is often linked to a theology in which the survivor is urged to forgive the perpetrator and not to take remedial action against him.

Such a theology is deficient in several respects. First, in the context of abuse, to make forgiveness the top priority seems perverse when the welfare and safety of the person being abused are at stake. It may be asked what lies behind such demands. If a desire to safeguard the permanence of a marriage is the motive, this is a displacement of responsibility: it is the perpetrator not the survivor who is endangering the relationship.

Second, it treats forgiveness *one-sidedly*, from the agency of the victim rather than the perpetrator. Although forgiveness is something freely offered, forgiving is a relational event which in order to be complete requires a response from the perpetrator. In Christian thought genuine acceptance of forgiveness involves repentance by the perpetrator, which embraces both admission of wrongdoing and sincere and realistic determination to act differently in the future.

None of this is likely to happen easily or quickly, and there may be considerable doubts about either the intention or the ability of the perpetrator to repent. About half of perpetrators make a verbal apology to their victims, and frequently offer gifts in compensation, but it is much rarer for this to be reflected in their ongoing behaviour. Overlooking this once again puts an unfair burden of responsibility on the survivor.

Third, it tends to treat forgiveness as an *isolated event*, unrelated to the whole pattern and history of relationships. It therefore obscures the extent to which forgiveness, when achievable, is a complex and messy process of coming to terms with the destructive consequences of past behaviour.

Fourth, forgiveness as a positive response by the survivor does not sideline the issue of justice. The offer of forgiveness by a survivor, and even its acceptance by the perpetrator, does not settle the question of appropriate punishment or reparation through which the perpetrator may be held to account.

Survivors of abuse must be allowed to come to terms with the issue of forgiveness in their own time and in their own way. That issue must not be allowed to eclipse the priorities of protecting the vulnerable and doing justice. The CTBI report on sexual abuse, *Time for Action*, suggests that churches need to repent and seek forgiveness from survivors for their unresponsiveness to stories of abuse.

It is of first importance for churches to offer sympathy and support to survivors of abuse and not to obstruct the provision of protection and the pursuit of justice.

A1.7   Correcting theology

When as Christians we recognize the presence and impact of harmful theology, the only proper response is to correct it in ways which are truthful and life-giving. Sometimes this is like the correction of the course of a boat, adjusting the steering and turning the rudder in order to proceed in the right direction; at other times it involves a complete reorientation and turnaround. The Church's response to domestic abuse calls for some fairly radical corrections at certain points.

In undertaking this we seek the guidance of the Holy Spirit, who is described in John 14–16 as the Spirit of truth and life, defined by the character of Jesus. The negative aspect of this guidance is that the Spirit convicts us of actions and attitudes which are wrong or life-denying, enabling us to discern the difference between the purpose of God and what stands in opposition to it.

Part of the Spirit's function is to help the Christian community to interpret the Bible and tradition in the light of 'what belongs to Jesus' (John 16.15), so that we may sift the healthy from the unhealthy elements of our inheritance and be 'guided into all the truth' (John 16.13). This critical and creative activity continues in openness to the presence of God in the unfolding history of the world ('the things that are to come'), and calls Christians to attend carefully to testimony both within and beyond the life of the Church. The production of these guidelines can be seen as one small moment in the corrective process – and obviously not the last word.

Theological correction requires critical awareness both of ideas which are being expressed and the context in which they are expressed. It must extend not only to sermons and formal teaching, but also to the use of hymns, symbols and metaphors, and the everyday actions which are informed by belief in God. It also calls for imagination and sensitivity in using potentially problematic language and doctrines without losing hold of the truth which they are able to convey.

For example, the idea of God as 'Lord' *may* be used in harsh and domineering ways. However, it expresses a truth about the character of God and the proper human response of worship and service which must not be lost. The theology of St Paul (who is often unfairly portrayed as an authoritarian and a misogynist) is helpful at this point. Paul was constrained by his experience of Christ to interpret Lordship in terms of grace and self-giving love. If *Jesus* is Lord, then the character of God's authority which he mediates to us is not demeaning but affirming; not oppressive but liberating; and not disabling but empowering. His power is at the service of the weak and vulnerable, and stands in judgement on all abuse and violence.

Keeping this pattern at the heart of all our praying, thinking, relating and teaching will displace harmful theology and give space for the Church to take its bearings from the 'breadth and length and height and depth' of God's love made known in Christ (Ephesians 3.18). The authentic human expression of that love is set out powerfully and memorably in 1 Corinthians 13.4–7. We cannot read and meditate on that text too often.

> Love is patient; love is kind; love is not envious or boastful or arrogant or rude. It does not insist on its own way; it is not irritable or resentful; it does not rejoice in wrongdoing, but rejoices in the truth. It bears all things, believes all things, hopes all things, endures all things.

That kind of theology should inform and guide all our relationships, both helping to prevent domestic abuse and equipping us to deal with it rightly when it occurs. As Jesus says following the act of foot-washing which enacts his role as both Servant and Lord, 'If you know these things, you are blessed if you *do* them' (John 13.17).

Appendix 2
Challenging myths, excuses and denial

Society and churches have traditionally found all sorts of ways not to 'own' the problem of domestic abuse. Here are some common examples:

A2.1 Denying that the problem exists

'We don't have that sort of thing in our parish.'

Domestic abuse affects people of every kind of background and faith and creed and culture and location and wealth. Even the smallest and richest villages will contain survivors of abuse and violence, perhaps wealthy, perhaps pillars of the community. Our stereotypes are incorrect.

Victims of abuse within a same-sex relationship are likely to face denial at two levels. They may experience a negative response to their partnership, not least within a church community, which will make it especially difficult for them to disclose abuse with the expectation of a sympathetic reception.

A2.2 Blaming the victim

'Why did they pick them in the first place? This is their decision, we don't have to deal with it.'

There are countless identical accounts given by survivors, saying, 'I don't understand what happened – it was an ideal relationship, then I became pregnant and it was like they became a different person overnight – from generous and caring to obsessive, controlling, abusive and violent. I thought I was going mad – that no one would ever believe me because they were still loving and "normal" in public, and sometimes there are good weeks at home, then it's back to a living hell again for no reason.'

Abusers often repeat their behaviour from one relationship to another. It is not the fault of their partners, and neither is it yet normally possible for their partners or any outsiders or friends to spot them in advance. There is usually no sinister expression, no general nasty nature and their public lives can be exemplary. They are often described as 'charmers'. They are brilliant at hiding this alter ego and often shower prospective partners with affection.

Likewise, survivors may have become skilled at disguising how they feel, how scared and desperate and/or in pain they are.

'Surely she must have done something to cause it.'

Victims of abuse have invariably done nothing at all. No one deserves abuse. No one deserves a black eye or a broken rib because they didn't get the dinner on the table in time.

An abusive individual will usually try to pick apart every single action of their partner as a way of controlling them, no matter what they do or don't do.

'Oh come on, it wasn't that serious. I've been in arguments and I didn't fall apart did I? You need some perspective!'

It is sometimes tempting to minimize the survivor's experiences. After all (we might wrongly reason), we've all been in arguments, so if they can't cope, then it's their problem. Yet an abusive relationship is not about an ordinary, everyday argument in which both people have a bit of a yell and then make up. It is very different indeed and often involves repeated behaviour. We must guard against deciding which abusive behaviour is worth bothering with, and which is not. We must offer help and support to all who ask for and need it.

'Why don't they just leave? Or report it to the police? If they choose to stay, it's not our problem, is it? They went back again, so it's their choice.'

This is a response we must challenge as a Church. What other crime in the world *requires* the victim to be the one to leave home? It's not a normal response to people disclosing burglary or arson or vandalism or harassment from strangers, but it is often our standard response to those who experience the crime of domestic abuse in the home.

Leaving is far from an easy solution to a very, very complex problem. Those who leave home often have to leave behind all they have – friends, family, neighbours, schools, clothes, photos, gardens, pets – everything they've worked their whole life to achieve, and rebuild a life when they are already exhausted, depressed, anxious, demoralized and often injured. It is no small matter to walk out, let alone when children are involved too. In addition, leaving does not always end the abuse. It may end the relationship but may increase the abuse. In many cases for women, the most dangerous time is immediately after separation, when the violent partner is angry at losing 'control' of their family. This is especially hazardous in some minority ethnic groups where it is seen as dishonourable to leave the family for *any* reason.

As a church, we need to focus on what is possible and *safe* for that person and their children, not on our own expectations for the couple or individual. We must not assume that God will heal the relationship in the way we want it to be healed.

'You're just exhausted and not thinking straight, you just need a rest or a break and you'll see things differently then. (*I think she's a bit unstable, the poor dear*).'

Many survivors of domestic abuse become depressed, anxious or suffer from other mental health issues because of abusive behaviour towards them. It does not mean they are not telling the truth: indeed, it may well be further evidence of the truth of the abusive behaviour.

'If you can't cope with being in the same church as your partner, maybe you should leave until you feel strong enough to come back.'

If people are still together in an abusive relationship, there are real issues about how to handle the situation in church and in support groups. Survivors should not be expected to leave a source of support. It might take some careful thought and planning, but people should not be expected to change support groups or church services unless it is for the safety of others (see Appendix 5 on the needs of survivors).

A2.3   Excusing the conduct of the perpetrator

'But I know the partner . . . they're a good person . . . they've had a really bad childhood . . . they're just a bit down, that's all . . . they didn't mean it . . . it's just they had a bit to drink . . . it was just a row that went a bit far . . . he said she was nagging him and you know what a nagging wife can be like, eh?'

There are no excuses for abusive behaviour. Domestic abuse is always wrong, whatever the circumstances. There is a temptation to try to avoid hearing things that are uncomfortable or do not fit with our own experience. As has been already said, abusers can be charming and persuasive and can find plausible excuses if accused of abusive behaviour. It is acceptable for the person who is listening to be unsure of the truth. However, those who disclose must still be heard with respect in accordance with the guidelines. We must not automatically seek to disbelieve the survivor or automatically look to excuse the perpetrator.

A2.4   Excusing our own behaviour

'It's not my problem. I'm too busy. I'm not an expert. It's not our job to cope with this. I might make it worse.'

The whole process of denial, minimizing, excusing and 'blaming the victim' is common throughout society. It is immensely damaging for survivors, and does nothing to help or change the perpetrator, who needs specialist intervention from domestic abuse perpetrator projects (see Appendix 9) if he is to change the way he behaves.

We are called as a church to respond appropriately to abusive behaviour, no matter how hard it is for us, and we must learn to watch out for and challenge excuses and denial. It is never wrong to listen with respect and caring, and to put a survivor or perpetrator in touch with the right services to help them.

'Surely it couldn't have happened to him? What sort of a wimp is he?'

Although all survivors of domestic abuse face challenges of disclosure and being believed, the complicating issue of embarrassment may *also* preclude a male partner from disclosing abuse to anyone. Whilst disclosure is never easy, men generally find it harder to talk about such issues, and society generally expects men to be 'tough enough to withstand anything'. They may find their emotions all the more difficult to come to terms with because society assumes all men are always tough and don't need to cry.

The threat of losing all or most contact with children can be a major hold on a male victim, keeping them tied to an abusive partner. They also have to battle through appeals to the Christian nature of marriage, but often attract additional blame for failing to hold the marriage together as the head of the household.

The church must be sensitive to the needs of men subjected to abuse and foster a culture in which they are given permission to share their pain with acceptance and no fear of ridicule or judgement.

A2.5   Racial and cultural myths

'Asian women have a higher tolerance level of domestic abuse.'

Domestic violence occurs in all religions, cultures and communities, but the pressures to remain silent may be more intense in some communities than others. Many minority women have to contend with tight-knit family and community structures, powerful notions of 'honour' and 'shame', and racism and discrimination in the wider society, all of which compel them to stay longer in an abusive relationship.

'Arranged marriage is the cause of domestic violence.'

The high incidence of domestic violence in the wider society challenges the assumption that domestic violence is more prevalent in minority communities where arranged marriage is practised. Domestic violence is not caused by arranged marriages: it is essentially about the maintenance of patriarchal power and privilege, which may present in different cultural forms in different communities.

Appendix 3
Legal considerations

People suffering violence, harassment or abuse in the home can seek protection from the **police** or through the **family courts**. The exact nature of the protection that will be appropriate will depend upon the circumstances of each particular case. There may then be a wealth of other ramifications, including housing, divorce, children, etc. In most cases, both victim and perpetrator will have to obtain specialist advice that is clearly outside the remit of a pastoral carer.

A3.1   What, then, should the person with pastoral responsibility do?

It is extremely important that victims are advised to:

● Consider reporting incidents of domestic abuse or harassment to the police, their GP, social worker and other independent third parties in order that an independent record of such events is maintained.

● Seek legal advice as soon as possible after incidents have occurred. Often, the availability of legal aid and emergency protection from the family courts depends upon action being taken swiftly. If the victim is not prepared to involve the police, it is still worth obtaining legal advice. A lack of information – or the provision of the wrong information – can result in a victim feeling that she/he has no options for action, which rarely proves correct.

Each police station should have officers who have received special training dedicated to dealing with situations of domestic abuse. It is well worth forging links directly with such people.

A3.2   What are the options for the victim?

Essentially **the police** act as the primary source for assistance in acute situations. The police can make arrests for assault or other criminal offences as they see fit. They can also make arrests for harassment under the **Protection from Harassment Act**. A person does not have to have been the victim of physical assault in order to be suffering from such harassment.

However, a victim may not want to involve the police. If this were the case, there are other options available from the **family court** that can afford personal protection. This will entail obtaining specialist legal advice from a family solicitor.

Emergency action can also involve regulating the contact between a parent and children if it is deemed to be in the children's best interests.

A3.3   The legal framework

If the police make an arrest following an incident of domestic abuse, they can prescribe **bail conditions** to keep an alleged offender away from the victim and the family whilst investigations continue or whilst a trial is pending.

The family courts can make two kinds of court order to protect victims:

- **A Non-Molestation Order** prevents a person from threatening, assaulting, harassing or intimidating another.

- **An Occupation Order** either can force the alleged offender to leave the home or can allow someone who has been forcibly ejected from his/her home to return.

In emergency situations, these orders can be obtained within 24 hours and without notice being given to the alleged offender. It is important to note that in practice these may not be very effective.

In cases where there has been a history of violence or the threat of violence, either order can be backed with a **power of arrest** so that the police can arrest someone who is in breach of the order regardless of whether that person has committed a criminal offence. That person will then be brought back to the court and can be fined or imprisoned if the breach is proved.

Public Legal Funding ('Legal Aid')

It is right to say that legal advice is often expensive, and this may in itself be a disincentive to a victim. However, in many cases public funding may be available to obtain advice and, if necessary, to apply to court for the orders mentioned above. Such availability will depend upon the person's financial means and the circumstances of the case. Solicitors that conduct family legal aid work are likely to advertise the fact in any Yellow Pages listing or equivalent. Most will also have a solicitor or caseworker dedicated to domestic violence cases.

Information sharing and confidentiality

General duty of confidentiality[21]

Both law and sound morals impose a general duty not to pass on information which has been received in the clear expectation that it will be treated in confidence. That duty is not absolute, however, and the courts will not intervene to restrain disclosure where (a) the information relates to a crime or other serious misconduct and (b) disclosure is in the public interest. **Thus, where a victim is judged to be at risk of significant harm or an adult is likely to harm themselves or others, usually it will be legally possible, appropriate and highly desirable to disclose relevant information to the public authorities for the sake of protecting that vulnerable adult.**

If such information has been received in confidence, the person giving the information should in the first instance be encouraged to disclose it to the authorities him or herself. Alternatively, the person receiving the disclosure should ask permission to pass the information on. If this request is denied it might still be possible to pass the information to a statutory body. Government guidance relating to child protection issued in 2003 gives helpful advice, which is also relevant in the context of the protection of vulnerable adults. It states:

Disclosure in the absence of consent[22]

The law recognizes that disclosure of confidential information without consent or a court order may be justified in the public interest to prevent harm to others.

The key factor in deciding whether to disclose confidential information is proportionality: is the proposed disclosure a proportionate response to the need to protect the welfare of the child? The amount of confidential information disclosed, and the number of people to whom it is disclosed, should be no more than is strictly necessary to meet the public interest in protecting the health and well-being of a child. The more sensitive the information is, the greater the child-focused need must be to justify disclosure and the greater the need to ensure that only those professionals who have to be informed receive the material.

Confession

It is possible that relevant information may be disclosed in the particular context of confession. Canon law constrains a priest from disclosing details of any crime or offence which is revealed in the course of formal confession: however, there is some doubt as to whether this absolute privilege is consistent with the civil law.[23] Where a penitent's own behaviour is at issue, the priest should not only urge the person to report it to the police or social services, but may judge it necessary to withhold absolution until this evidence of repentance has been demonstrated. It is in everyone's interest to recognize the distinction between what is heard in formal confession (however this might take place) which is made for the quieting of conscience and intended to lead to absolution, and disclosures made in pastoral situations. For this reason, it is helpful if confessions are normally heard at advertised times or by other arrangement or in some way differentiated from a general pastoral conversation or a meeting for spiritual direction.

Relevant legislation

Legislation designed to safeguard the private lives of individuals has been framed to take account of the overriding need to protect the wider community against crime and serious misconduct. Nevertheless, it is important to be aware of the legal obligations, which apply to those who hold sensitive information about others.

Data protection

Information which relates to an individual's physical or mental health, sexual life or to the commission or alleged commission of an offence is treated as sensitive personal data for the purposes of the Data Protection Act 1998. The Act restricts the use of such information, including its disclosure to third parties, without the explicit consent of the individual concerned. However, there is a provision which permits the processing of sensitive personal data where the individual cannot give consent, providing that the processing is necessary for the provision of confidential counselling, advice, support or any other service.[24] There is also an exemption which permits disclosure of personal information to the police where that disclosure is made for the purposes of preventing or detecting crime.[25]

Human rights

The Human Rights Act 1998 incorporated into UK law the European Convention on Human Rights, so that it is now unlawful for a public authority to act in contravention of a Convention right.

What constitutes a 'public authority' for the purposes of the 1998 Act is a developing area of the law. The most recent judicial opinion[26] suggests that (except in cases such as the conduct of a marriage where the minister can be said to be exercising a governmental function in a broad sense) a person carrying out duties within the Church of England which are simply part of the mission of the Church (such as pastoral care) is not acting as a public authority. However, this is an area on which advice should be sought from the diocesan registrar in any particular case.

Article 8 of the Convention provides that everyone has the right to respect for his private and family life, his home and his correspondence, and that a public authority may only interfere with this right where such interference is lawful and necessary for certain purposes. The most relevant of those in the child protection context are the prevention of disorder or crime, the protection of health or morals and the protection of the rights and freedoms of others. In any circumstances where Article 8 applies to a public body, there is a judgement to be made as to whether, on balance, an interference with that right by a public authority can be justified. Where allegations of abuse are concerned, the potential harm that might result from not reporting such allegations will be a relevant factor.

Freedom of information

No Church body is a public authority for the purpose of the Freedom of Information Act 2000, and so the Act does not have any direct impact upon the Church's activities. However, those sharing information with public authorities (such as local government departments and agencies) should be aware that those bodies are subject to the Act. However, information held by a public authority in connection with investigations and legal proceedings is generally exempt from public disclosure under the Act.

Appendix 4
Needs of children and young people

I never knew what to expect when I came in from school. The silences, the place wrecked, tears, the constant questioning . . . we couldn't take anyone home because it would cause a huge row and my other parent would get yelled at or worse for hour after hour because of it. We couldn't go out anywhere either. I had panic attacks and I just wanted to kill myself. There was no one to talk to. No one cared except 'X' and they just didn't know what to do.

(Account from a survivor who had witnessed domestic abuse for the whole of their childhood.)

The NSPCC guide
http://www.nspcc.org.uk/inform/ConferenceReports/ForgetMeNot/Domestic
ViolenceAndAbuse.ppt
is a good resource to introduce people to the impact of domestic abuse on children.

A4.1   Impact

Witnessing or overhearing domestic abuse is now considered a form of child abuse by the perpetrator of the violent/abusive behaviour. Children have been largely forgotten victims of domestic abuse and sometimes their voices are not heard.

The short and long-term impact on children is extensive, often affects them in adult life and can include the following:

- Being hurt themselves, either deliberately or when they are trying to stop one parent from hurting the other.

- Being frightened by seeing physical violence and/or abusive arguments.

- Blaming themselves for the behaviour because they were not good enough or strong enough.

- Children often lose their childhood because they have to take on a caring role for siblings if parents become unreliable.

- It can make young children really scared of the abuser and other people of the same gender.

- Young children can be less able to talk about the experience and more likely to be caught in the middle because of their dependence on their caregivers.

- Young children can exhibit behaviour such as being very demanding; bed wetting; being clingy; crying a lot; not sleeping; not eating well; developing more slowly; becoming babyish; and being aggressive to other children or their parents.

- In contrast some children may become overly anxious to please, unnaturally well-behaved, which is less easily detected and can meet with approval rather than concern.

- Older children may become violent, aggressive, suicidal or anorexic; fail to do well at school; refuse to go to school because they don't want to leave the victim; suffer anxiety attacks; run away from home; find it difficult to make friends or take friends home; become attention seekers; turn to drugs or alcohol as a way of coping.

- Children and young people may become afraid of their own emotions such as anger.

- Children and young people may have difficulty in creating positive affirming relationships particularly in adult life.

A4.2   Needs

When children have been asked what they need, they are very clear and very consistent:

- Someone appropriate to talk to outside of the family who will listen to their concerns and be able to help them.

- Safety for them and the rest of their family away from the danger, some space to recover.

- A voice in legal matters such as child contact. After parents separate, the *child* is the one with rights to good contact with a loving, safe parent. The parents' rights are subject to the child's best interests and child protection issues have to be taken into consideration.

- Reassurance that professionals in the case such as social workers, Children and Family Court Reporters (CAFCASS) or child psychiatrists will know enough about the topic, and that their fears and experiences will not be dismissed. In particular, research has shown that children rarely disclose what has happened to them in a first interview and it may take a long time for them to trust someone enough to disclose abusive behaviour.

- Someone to pick up their behaviour, injuries or absence at school.

- Play. Some local groups offer therapy through play.

Children are more aware of problems than their parents realize, but they do not always understand the reasons. They want their parents to be well and happy and safe. They fear never knowing what mood the abusive parent will be in, whether they will be nice or nasty today. There may not be time or safety enough for them to have a normal childhood, but instead they have to be quiet and invisible so as not to cause problems for one parent if they do or say something wrong. They often suffer from social isolation as it's too risky to bring anyone home in case it sparks violence later, or because they are too afraid or depressed to want to play.

Children need sensitive pastoral care from clergy, youth leaders and children's workers, for example, not talk about 'broken homes' or 'complete' or 'happy' families. Children may feel guilty too and may be facing the reality that a loved parent or carer is also an abuser. They too may have absorbed the view that 'Mummy deserved it.' Family Services can be hell for them with prayers like 'Thank you Father for all the happiness that families can share.'

A4.3 Separation and contact difficulties

The problem of abusive situations does not disappear if parents separate. Child contact can become another opportunity for the child and the resident parent to experience new abusive situations. The most likely time for a woman to be murdered is at the point of separation. This has not been shown to be a factor in cases where the man leaves an abusive wife and takes the children.

In cases of domestic abuse allegations and separation, children can becomes weapons of the abuser (who perhaps wants revenge as well as contact) in hostile, long and expensive civil court cases concerning custody, or 'residence' matters. The strain on children and the non-abusive parent can be insurmountable. Children's voices are not yet well heard in many such cases. Those supporting children should be aware of these challenges and strains on children.

Because families and friends take sides on separation, many children and young people lose contact with half of their extended family because grandparents, for example, find it hard to cope with if their son or daughter is accused of domestic abuse.

A4.4 What to say and do

See Appendix 3 for what to do if you become aware of a child disclosing that they are in a household in which there is domestic abuse.

If you are in any doubt, seek advice from the person who is responsible for child protection in the parish or diocese, the social services or a specialist agency such as NSPCC, or via Women's Aid or Refuge as to the correct course of action. Do not speak directly to the alleged abuser or pass on what the child has disclosed. This could put the child in danger. You should not attempt to investigate the situation yourself. Continue to support the child and seek support for yourself too.

Disclosures from children:

- Must be listened to carefully, avoiding the use of leading questions. You must let the child be the one to decide what to tell, whom to tell it to in the church, and when. Forcing a child to tell, or expecting them to tell a stranger on first meeting, is not appropriate or productive. You might want to ask them how they feel about the situation, and ask what they would like to happen. You can't promise to keep what they tell you confidential, though. If they disclose something that is a child protection risk, you cannot agree not to tell anyone else, as this is against both the law and common sense. You can, however, help them to understand that people are going to try to help them, not make it worse for them.

- Must be taken seriously.

- Must be acted upon in accordance with the child protection policy of your church and by reference to the *Protecting all God's Children* policy.

- Must be carefully recorded as soon as possible (seeking to quote the discloser rather than the recipient's interpretations) and kept in a safe place.

Appendix 5

Needs of survivors – a survivor's perspective

A5.1   Needs on disclosure

- Respectful listening, talking and reassurance form the basis of appropriate pastoral care. In many ways it is a multiple and complex loss or bereavement with many of the same emotions attached and the same exhaustion and loss of confidence.

- Survivors are in control of their decisions and options. They need to lead rather than be told what to do and need to choose the person they talk to. Considerations such as gender and age need to be taken into account.

- People begin to move from victim to survivor when they are believed and not blamed, when they begin not to take responsibility for the abuser's behaviour.

- Trust takes time to build. Survivors may disclose little by little.

- Survivors might need support in telling the children's school, family members such as grandparents, and the church about what is happening.

Practical needs might include

- A safe place, protection and medical attention.

- A safety plan, including personal safety devices (e.g. alarm, mobile phone, improved locks) – obtainable from the police or community care schemes.

- A list of items to take with them, e.g. money, birth and marriage certificates, passports, benefit books, chequebooks, address book containing names and addresses of friends and family, children's favourite toys.

- Expert professional help.

- Childcare while seeking help.

- DIY assistance, e.g. mending windows.

- Furniture, household and baby equipment, toys, etc. in cases of rehousing.

- Care for pets.

- Advocacy and support during the legal or financial processes such as getting benefits.

Longer-term pastoral and support needs

- Continued interest, care and support are needed, as leaving is a bereavement and takes years to get over. Sometimes people return to abusive partners, or young singles move back into abusive homes, out of loneliness, isolation or sexual need.

- All abuse robs people of healthy self-esteem and sexual confidence. Abusers often repeatedly tell victims that they are sexually unattractive and no one else will want them. This can have two effects on survivors in future sexual relationships – a need to prove that wrong, or a lasting belief that it is right. Talking with others, either fellow survivors or sensitive friends, in open honest discussion enables recovery and may avoid repeating patterns.

- Survivors need more support than just Christian groups, and their experiences have to be worked through or may cause serious problems in later life, including repeating patterns.

- Survivors should be encouraged to take up post-trauma services for adults, children and young people. Counselling, group and play therapy are offered by many domestic abuse organizations. Fear, anxiety, loneliness, a deep sense of failure, sexual longing and despair about one's attractiveness or adequacy are all long-term outcomes, and a safe place to acknowledge these powerful emotions is needed.

- 'Disclosure anxiety' and sense of guilt afflicts survivors sometimes for a lifetime as the social sanctions against 'telling' are powerful, especially in Christian contexts of honouring parents, loving and forgiving relatives, even abusive ones.

- Self-esteem, assertiveness training and counselling are vital if the survivor is to avoid future abusive relationships. Sometimes a conversion or spiritual reawakening accompanies an escape, especially if Christians have proved supportive. It is easy to say, 'All that's past now and things will be different', and not to deal with the underlying attitudes and childhood scripts of both adult and child victims that allow abuse to occur.

- Support is needed from the wider community, particularly if the perpetrator is a key member of a church community. There are likely to be many confused feelings around, including shock, disbelief and people's affection for the perpetrator. Help is needed in making sense of the situation and sorting out issues. Openness is crucial, especially with the abuser, as all abuse thrives on secrecy and misplaced 'confidentiality'.

Appendix 6

Experiences of women in black and minority ethnic communities[27]

The experience of those who work with minority women shows that in South Asian communities, where family and community structures remain strong and where marriage is the only legitimate site of female existence, women are likely to tolerate violence and abuse for longer periods than either their white or black African or Caribbean counterparts. Indian, Pakistani and Bangladeshi women are more likely than black African or Caribbean women to be married. Family structures are changing in the various Asian communities, but many remain tight-knit and this can serve as an additional barrier to reporting violence. Black African and Caribbean women, on the other hand, are more likely to head single households, but less likely to report domestic violence to agencies such as the police due to experiences and perceptions of institutional racism.

Culturally specific forms of violence and abuse such as forced marriage, honour crimes, honour killings, female genital mutilation, child and women abuse related to 'possession by evil spirits' or 'dowry problems' must be addressed within the framework of domestic violence, since the need to protect remains the main imperative, irrespective of the cultural context in which domestic violence occurs. Such forms of abuse are common across the various religious communities and are often justified by religious and cultural beliefs as a way of maintaining patriarchal power and control. Often the violence is perpetrated by members of the extended family, with the collusion of others in the community.

It is crucial that we understand concepts of shame and honour in South Asian and many other minority communities as obstacles to women's attempts to escape violence and abuse. Pressures to conform to traditional roles and to maintain the honour of family and community usually rest on women and their behaviour. They are expected to remain silent in the face of abuse in order to preserve their family honour. Reporting violence can impair the marriage prospects of their children and their siblings and affect their status in the community. They may be cut off from their close and extended family, the base of their social and emotional life. Behaviour which is perceived to deviate from cultural norms is often punished in a variety of ways ranging from ostracism to 'honour killings'. The pressure to maintain family or community honour can be so intense that many women contemplate, attempt or commit suicide rather than report violence or seek outside help. Research shows that rates of suicide and self-harm are up to three times higher for South Asian women than for women in the wider society.

Whilst many of the common myths and assumptions about domestic violence and women in the wider society are also applicable to minority women, such women have extra constraining factors to overcome due to their race and gender. These act as barriers within and outside the community.

Within the community, the following act as obstacles:

- patriarchal structures and sexual discrimination;

- tight-knit families and communities where the religious and community leadership is conservative, women have limited public visibility and the incidence of sexual discrimination is high;

- notions of honour and shame which are strongly held features of family and community existence;

- lack of alternative safe havens, where women are not judged or condemned for leaving violent relationships;

- lack of recognition of the fundamental rights of women and children to life, liberty and freedom from being subject to torture or inhuman or degrading treatment.

Outside the communities, the following act as obstacles:

- racial discrimination;

- racial violence;

- inability to access services and support due to language difficulties and isolation;

- lack of specialist facilities for minority women;

- the dominance of the 'multicultural approach' which can amount to non-intervention on grounds of respect for 'cultural sensitivity';[28]

- insecure immigration and asylum status.

In addition the Southall Black Sisters raise concern about the use of mediation and reconciliation by service providers in resolving family disputes (see also Appendix 9 on working with perpetrators), particularly with women and young persons from cultural backgrounds where mediation with the aim of reconciliation is already practised. Mediation can have a role to play where marital tensions exist, but only in contexts where the partners or family members occupy a more equal playing field and where is there is no risk of violence or abuse. In the vast majority of cases, women from minority communities have usually undergone several (almost always failed) attempts at reconciliation following informal methods of resolution involving family or community elders. The reasons for the high rates of failure are to do with the fact that the family structures and community dynamics in many minority communities are built on unequal power relations between men and women legitimized by cultural or religious practice. In community-based mediation processes, women are rarely heard and even where they are, they are blamed and made to feel guilty for the disintegration of their marriage or family. In such circumstances, women have little or no right to assert their own wishes and desires.

In many cases, women are lulled into a false sense of security by community elders or family members promising to protect and intervene if future problems occur, only to be subject to even greater controls and restrictions and/or punished through violence and other means. In more extreme cases, following mediation, women have been maimed, abducted or killed for having brought dishonour to their families and communities.

Mediation as an option or alternative to utilizing the civil law can therefore be a highly dangerous practice. The Foreign and Commonwealth Office, the Association of Police Officers (ACPO), the Home Office and other government departments, including those responsible for social services, have warned against mediation and reconciliation in their guidance on forced marriage. This warning is equally applicable to all forms of violence and abuse experienced by black and minority women.

The ramifications of mediation and reconciliation within different cultures must therefore be better understood so that it does not add to the pressures that women are already facing to 'save' their marriage. Adopting standards or approaches which deviate from what is good practice in the wider community in respect of domestic violence, will have a discriminatory and unjust impact on women from minority communities.

Resources

Support and advice are available from a number of specialist organizations which can be found on the BBC web site (see p.15).

Southall Black Sisters
21 Avenue Road
Southall
Middlesex
UB1 3BL
Tel. 0208 571 9595
Monday to Friday, 10 a.m. to 5 p.m. Closed Wednesdays.
southallblacksisters@btconnect.com
http://www.southallblacksisters.org.uk

Elder abuse

Abuse of older people is a hidden, and often ignored, problem in society. While the profile of child abuse has been raised in recent years a number of organizations and bodies have been responsible for reminding us of the particular needs and problems that can be associated with older people.

It is impossible to quantify how many older people are being abused at any one given time; it has been suggested that the number could be as large as 500,000. However, at the time of writing many people continue to be unaware of the problem and few measures have been taken to address it.

A7.1   Defining elder abuse

No standard definition of elder abuse applies within the UK public sector. The term itself has been imported from the USA. It has no legal status and would not be recognized by many older people.

Action on Elder Abuse has produced the following outline summary of elder abuse:

> **Elder abuse is the mistreatment of an older person.**

Who is abused?

Both older men and women can be at risk of being abused.

Are there different kinds of abuse?

People can be abused in different ways. These include:
physical abuse; psychological abuse; financial abuse; sexual abuse; neglect; inappropriate use of medication.

Where does abuse happen?

Abuse can occur anywhere:
someone's own home; a carer's home; day care; residential care; a nursing home; hospital.

Who abuses?

The abuser is usually well-known to the person being abused. They may be:
a partner, child or relative; a friend or neighbour; a paid or volunteer care worker; a health or social worker, or other professional.

Older people may also be abused by a person they care for.

Why does it happen?

There are many reasons why abuse occurs and these may vary with each incident. Many of its causes are not yet fully understood. Abuse may range from a spontaneous act of frustration to systematic premeditated assaults on an older person.

At home some of the causes would appear to include:

poor-quality long-term relationships; a carer's inability to provide the level of care required; a carer with mental or physical health problems.

In other settings abuse may be a symptom of a poorly run establishment.

It is likely to occur when staff are:

inadequately trained; poorly supervised; have little support from management; or work in isolation.

A7.2   Pastoral and practical responses

Given the complex nature of this subject any individual or group would do well to seek further advice and training. A list of responses is contained at the end of this Appendix. It is also important to put this issue into a pastoral context whereby some of the reasons why relationships break down and problems occur might be balanced alongside appropriate responses.[29]

What to do and who to contact

If you are being abused or are concerned about someone you know, it is important that you talk it through with someone. You should be aware that, despite your concern, any older person has the right to decline assistance.

Support and information is available from Action on Elder Abuse through its helpline:

Elder Abuse Response
Tel. 080 8808 8141
Monday to Friday, 10 a.m. to 4.30 p.m.

If you feel that the problem is very serious and warrants immediate action (e.g. if a person is at immediate risk of harm) you should contact the police. In an emergency you should dial 999.

A few resources

Action on Elder Abuse aims to prevent abuse in old age by raising awareness, education, promoting research and the collection and dissemination of information.

Action on Elder Abuse
Astral House
1268 London Road
London
SW16 4ER
aea@ace.org.uk
http://www.elderabuse.org.uk
Elder Abuse Response helpline
Tel. 080 8808 8141

In addition to Action on Elder Abuse there are a number of organizations that may help when an older person is being abused:

Age Concern
FREEPOST (SWB 30375)
Ashburton
Devon
TQ13 7ZZ
Tel. 0800 009966
7 a.m. to 7 p.m.

Offers a series of fact sheets designed to provide practical information for older people to help themselves, and as a definitive guide for those whose work supports older people. Separate national organizations for England, Wales, Northern Ireland and Scotland. Local organizations and groups are listed in the telephone directory under Age Concern.

Carers National Association
10–25 Glasshouse Yard
London
EC1A 4JS
CarersLine: Tel. 080 8808 7777
10 a.m. to 12 p.m. and 2 p.m. to 4 p.m.

Provides advice, information and support for carers. In addition there are separate national organizations for Northern Ireland, Scotland and Wales.

Counsel and Care
Twyman House
16 Bonny Street
London
NW1 9PG
Advice line: Tel. 0845 300 7585
10.30 a.m. to 4 p.m.

Has particular expertise in residential and nursing care and runs an advice line for older people, their carers and relatives.

Public Concern at Work
Lincoln's Inn House
Kingsway
London
WC2B 6EN
Tel. 020 7404 6609
9 a.m. to 6 p.m.

A legal advice organization which can be contacted by those working with older people without breaching any terms of employment or duty of confidentiality.

The Relatives and Residents Association
5 Tavistock Place
London
WC1H 9SS
Information service telephone: 020 7916 6055
10 a.m. to 12.30 p.m. and 1.30 p.m. to 5 p.m.

For anyone with an older relative or friend in a care home or long-stay hospital. Provides a 'listening ear' and practical advice about problems.

Appendix 8
Marriage preparation

The principles of understanding humanity (female and male) as made in God's image and of equal worth; of equality amongst people and within relationships; of no condoning of any form of abuse should undergird any marriage preparation offered by the Church. Some theological ideas such as headship and submission models of men and women have been expressed in the liturgy in the past in the different promises expressed by the man and the woman.[30] However, as the Methodist report says[31] a promise to obey was in the past part of different standards or expectations of women and men within marriage, e.g. the fact that women had no standing in law until 1926. A mutuality expressed through the marriage partners being encouraged to be themselves rather than sticking to gendered roles offers a better interpretation of love and a better opportunity for both partners to grow and flourish in the relationship than does the differentiated model, in which one partner takes responsibility for the other's growth, but not vice versa.

Given the high incidence of domestic abuse within marriage, we recommend that clergy and lay people who offer marriage and wedding preparation should have attended some training on issues of domestic abuse. It is important that there is a clear understanding amongst those who offer marriage preparation that domestic abuse is always unacceptable and that domestic abuse breaks the sanctity of marriage.

There is considerable evidence that marriage can lead to the beginning or the escalation of domestic abuse, as it brings a heightened sense of 'ownership'. Marriage preparation offers an opportunity to challenge inappropriate behaviour and assumptions about domination, control or abuse, while making it clear that some degree of conflict within an intimate relationship is natural and healthy, if dealt with appropriately.

The subjects regularly dealt with when preparing couples for marriage, e.g. communication, conflict and in particular 'How do you deal with your anger?' offer an opportunity for couples to discuss together how their parents dealt with anger, rows and conflict or how the couple might have dealt with these in previous relationships. Sometimes those who have experienced domestic abuse as children have a very idealized view of marriage.[32]

It is possible that those working with couples hoping to marry may become aware or suspect that abuse is taking place or may take place between the partners. This is always a difficult area to deal with and illustrates the need for training for people involved in this work, but one or more of the following ideas might help in such a situation.

- The facilitator might include a statement at the beginning of the 'course' or conversation and again before dealing with a subject such as 'marital conflict' or anger. The following, which may need amending depending on the circumstances, is an example of a form of words that might be appropriate.

When we think about relationships in general and our own in particular, there is always a chance that issues may be raised that touch us in a way that leaves us feeling disturbed, uncomfortable or anxious. If this happens you may wish to speak to one of us today more privately or to seek help from a counsellor or other helping organization. We will hand out a resource list at the end of the day, which may be helpful.[33]

- If a domestic abuse issue is raised directly or indirectly by one of the couple, the facilitator should not pursue it in the presence of the other: this could be highly dangerous. They may need to find a way to give the person a chance to say more in private, with the object of encouraging them to get one-to-one help from a competent person or organization. Again, an available resource list is helpful.

Working with perpetrators

As noted on page 8, working with perpetrators to change their behaviour is a difficult and still relatively underdeveloped area of practice. The deep-rooted and systematically distorted character of abusive behaviour means that 'quick fixes' are not available. Attempts to engineer such solutions endanger survivors and are not helpful to the perpetrator: they risk offering what Dietrich Bonhoeffer identified as 'cheap grace'.

There is a growing consensus that acceptable perpetrator programmes should

- Focus on enabling perpetrators to understand and take responsibility for their behaviour.

- Address both cognitive and behavioural issues, challenging perpetrators' attitudes and beliefs and enabling them to learn and adopt new ways of relating.

- Be organized on an inter-agency basis.

- Be conducted through group work rather than one-to-one counselling.

- Be of long-term duration (a minimum of 75 hours over 30 weeks is cited by RESPECT).

- *Not* be expected to bring about change on their own.

The motives of perpetrators for agreeing to undertake programmes may be mixed. They should not entertain expectations of a 'cure' for abusive behaviour which will relieve them of responsibility. If the motive is primarily an instrumental one – to preserve or restore a relationship with a partner which has been undermined by abuse, or to gain access to children – the programme is unlikely to succeed.

Resistance to changes in behaviour can stem not only from the perpetrator but from his extended family, who may take his part against the survivor, thereby reinforcing his sense of self-justification.

If working with perpetrators presents huge difficulties and uncertainties for trained professionals, what then can the Church do?

As always, whatever it does must give priority to the safety of survivors (and of church workers and members).

The Church's role must be to reinforce whatever is done by others to help perpetrators address their abusive behaviour. In some cases, this may require leaving events to take their course, either through reporting to the police or by the provision of professional help. Perpetrators may also need help with alcohol or drug misuse, or mental health problems. Insofar as the Church can influence the perpetrator it should encourage a realistic approach to recognizing personal need and seeking appropriate help.

Perpetrators should not be advised to deal with their behaviour through mediation, couple counselling or anger management. These methods are generally recognized to be ineffective and sometimes counterproductive.

If the perpetrator is a member of the Church, and the abuse has fallen short of criminal behaviour, a local congregation may be able to help by combining rejection of the abusive behaviour with a measure of personal acceptance. The model of 'support and accountability' embodied by the Circles of volunteers who monitor released sex offenders may sometimes be appropriate.[34]

If, however, the survivor is also a member of the local congregation, priority must be given to meeting their needs. The Church may feel obliged to provide for the spiritual needs and pastoral care of the perpetrator apart from the survivor. It may be worth exploring parallels to the setting of boundaries through supervision and guidelines which are recommended in some circumstances for congregations welcoming sex offenders into their midst.[35]

It may often be the case that the scope for constructive engagement with perpetrators is, tragically, limited. In dealing with them as human beings, church workers and congregations must not allow proper convictions about human worth and a naive belief in the possibility of change to lead them to overlook or condone abuse, or to compromise their responsibilities to protect and support survivors.

What if the abuser is a member of the clergy or another licensed minister?

If the partner of an ordained person is subjected to abuse, the issues of disclosure are very problematic. There have been a number of instances of abuse by clergy and other licensed ministers, and it is particularly important to apply the same guidelines to this situation as any other, because there may be a tendency to disbelieve the victim on account of the standing of the abuser within the church community. Clergy spouses should not be excluded from available support and resources.

If a clergy spouse who lives in church housing has decided to leave the relationship, they are likely to need alternative housing. Every diocesan bishop has appointed a Bishop's Visitor, whose role is to support the clergy spouse at the time of the breakdown of the marriage, and for as long as possible after, as the spouse needs. It is a role which involves giving information rather than professional advice. The Bishop's Visitor may be able to recommend and facilitate payment for counselling of clergy spouses who are survivors of abuse.

Under the new Clergy Discipline Measure (CDM), due to come into force in 2006, a priest sentenced to imprisonment for domestic abuse (including a suspended sentence), as for any offence may be removed from office and/or prohibited from exercising any functions as a priest (whether for life or for a fixed term).[36]

If a priest, on a marital break-up, is respondent to a petition for divorce or judicial separation based on unreasonable behaviour (which includes physical or mental abuse), then the bishop under the CDM will again have power, after consultation with the President of Tribunals, to remove the priest from office and /or impose a prohibition, without going through the normal complaints procedure.

The Bishop's Visitors' advice to bishops, 'Guidelines on Reinstatement', recommends that if a clergyperson applies for reinstatement following discipline or suspension, there shall be a process of consultation. This will normally begin only after a significant lapse of time from the offence, and with evidence of remorse and repentance. The consultation should wherever possible include the divorced or separated spouse. It may need to include others who have been most affected by the behaviour of the priest (such as children, close family members and parochial representatives). Wherever possible, the Bishop's Visitor who was involved at the time of the breakdown should also be consulted. It can be very upsetting for the survivor to see their abuser still in a position of authority and preaching about the love of God.

Broken Rites is an association of divorced and separated wives of clergy, ministers and Church Army Officers living in England, Wales, Scotland, Northern Ireland and the Republic of Ireland.

There is no prescribed complaints procedure against other non-ordained ministers, such as Readers, but the bishop has the power[37] to summarily revoke the licence in writing *'for any cause which appears to him to be good and reasonable, after having given the Reader sufficient opportunity of showing reason to the contrary'* — subject to a right of appeal by the Reader to the Archbishop of the Province.

Further details about this can be found in the forthcoming guidelines for those working with vulnerable adults, *Promoting a safe church*.

Appendix 11
Stories from survivors

All names and identifying details have been changed.

1. 'Linda' had been married to 'Stuart' for 4 years. He had been the perfect gentleman for the first year of their marriage, but she describes him as changing character the moment she first became pregnant. 'Things have got worse and worse, the tiniest thing will set him off. Not with other people, just with me. He starts punching and kicking things, smashing things in front of our son and I. He starts shouting and swearing and the more I try to calm it down the worse he is. He hit me so hard last year I had a miscarriage. Things were terrible last week. We went out for a lovely meal but when we got home he just went into a violent rage. I was so worried I tried to get our son out of the house to a friend, but he realized what I was trying to do, and he started shoving me. He snatched my cup of tea off me and smashed it, and then shoved me so hard against the wall saying I wasn't leaving the house . . . Our son was now crying and I pleaded with him to let me go but he just pushed me back with our son in my arms and pushed us out of the house and locked the door. He shouted that he'd kill me if I came back, and I really thought he meant it. I went round to my friend's house and I just didn't know what to do, I was so scared. That evening he kept calling me, pleading for me to go back home . . . promising me he'd never do it again. He was crying and said he wanted to end it all. I had nowhere else to go, and he sounded so ashamed that I ended up back at home and things were great for a few days. Now he's back to criticizing everything I do and blaming me for what he did and the violence has started up again and my friend says she won't help me because I went back to him. I don't know what to do, or who to go to for help. He has changed so much from how he was at the start. I used to love him so much. Now I am so scared of him.'

2. 'Alan' had been married to 'Julia' for ten years. He lived with emotional abuse and violence on a daily basis for most of this time, but felt that it wasn't right to hurt a woman even in self-defence. He felt trapped and isolated, felt to blame for not being man enough to sort it out. He felt as if he'd failed in his role as Christian 'Head of the Household'. 'If you share what has been happening with the minister/mutual friends/counsellor, I will count that as a personal betrayal and leave and you will never see the children again. . .You don't earn enough money to keep this family well-provided for. Call yourself a man . . . you're nothing but a big baby . . . that's right cry. That's all you're good for. Go on big baby, cry like the baby you are.'

3. 'Bez' has been married to 'Hal' for seven years. She explains, 'The first year we were together was wonderful, but then he started to get so jealous. Like, one day I was looking into the newsagent's window at the cards, when I looked round, he was staring at me and when we got home he yelled at me for hours and hours, saying it was because I must have fancied the guy at the

till. I was terrified to look at any men at all. He'd say he was sorry. After a year of this I was an emotional wreck, I even took an overdose because it was too much to cope with and I couldn't see any way out. He told me I was mad and it was all my fault. Now he's started to hit me. Last time it was in front of our five-year-old. I still have a black eye, but he says it doesn't count as domestic violence as he only pushed me into the banisters and it wasn't a punch. We have weeks when things are great and it's hard to remember the bad times. I still see that lovely man he used to be when it's good, but I'm so frightened when it's bad. He's a great dad, our child loves him. It's got to be my fault.'

4. 'Georgie' was living with 'Chaz' for 15 years. They had three girls of primary school age. He started off as a loving, caring partner until she fell pregnant. She lost the first baby through miscarriage and he blamed her totally, even though it wasn't her fault. Chaz expected Georgie to do everything for the children, hold down two part-time jobs, do every bit of the housework and also help him with his engineering projects way into the night. She was lucky if she got 6 hours of sleep a night for 12 of those years. When she fell desperately ill he still would not lift a finger to help but would yell at her until she dragged herself to look after the children. In hospital, he visited her only to take her more work to do. She was told every day that she was fat, stupid, ugly, useless, a hopeless mother, a wife who didn't ever care about him. She was kept away from friends and family 'because he should be all she needed', he told her. He checked her receipts, her phone calls, her post, her emails. She was kept desperately short of housekeeping money whilst he squandered his large salary on luxury goods. He was abusive to her in front of the children, who were terrified of him and wanted nothing to do with him, screaming and running away when he tried to take them from relatives one day, shaking like a leaf after contact sessions with him. He accused Georgie of making up all the abuse and turning the children against him, despite all of the witnesses who had seen his behaviour. Her opinion counted for nothing, and she struggled with depression and self-harm in absolute misery. He had an affair with a colleague, and this was the last straw for Georgie. She told him it had to stop, and how much she loved him but she'd have to leave if it kept going. He retaliated by reminding her that if she left, she would never see the kids again, and he'd tell everyone she was mad. Georgie contacted a Christian friend, who found the right information at church and put her in touch with Women's Aid. One of their refuge workers, and her friend, stood by her through four years of further hell after separation, in which Chaz then became violent to her, stalked her, threatened her repeatedly, took her to court endless times on made-up allegations which he dropped the moment she had got to the court room, but which terrified her and cost her a fortune to defend. He demanded to be given the children, and took her to court a further 15 times to see if he could get the children away from her. He told social services that she was an unfit mother, prompting a year of stressful investigation, which eventually backfired on him. Georgie and the children were left homeless at one point because he refused to pay the child support which was paying for the mortgage. She could have gone to a refuge with the children, but a Christian friend took them in.

Georgie's faith was shattered by all she had been through. She couldn't understand how a loving God could let her and the children endure all of this. That never deterred those who saw how much she and the children needed help. Those in the church had stood by relentlessly, praying for her, helping her in court, keeping her safe, keeping her in touch with people who were trained to help. She and the children are now truly safe, at last. They have a new small home of their own, and enough food on the table, and friends and family around them.

Notes

1 Some of these principles are taken from the value base of the Welcare Service in Southwark Diocese.

2 http://www.crimereduction.gov.uk/dv01.htm.

3 Kathryn Coleman, Celia Hird and David Povey, 'Violent Crime Overview, Homicide and Gun Crime 2004/2005', Home Office.

4 http://www.womensaid.org.uk/domestic-violence-survivors-handbook.asp?section=000100010008000100360002.

5 Sylvia Walby, *The Economic Cost of Domestic Violence*, The Women and Equality Unit DTI, 2004.

6 E. Stanko, 'The day to count: a snapshot of the impact of domestic violence in the UK', *Criminal Justice* 1.2 (February 2000), as quoted in *Domestic Abuse and the Methodist Church: Taking Action*, Methodist Publishing House, 2005, Section 1.3.

7 Stanko, 'The day to count'.

8 http://www.homeoffice.gov.uk/crime-victims/reducing-crime/domestic-violence.

9 J. Ogg and G. Bennett, 'Elder abuse in Britain', *British Medical Journal* 305, 24 October 1992, pp. 998–9.

10 Department of Health, 2003.

11 NCH, 1994.

12 'Women's Mental Health: Into the Mainstream', Department of Health, 2002.

13 Hilary Saunders, 'Twenty-nine child homicides: Lessons still to be learnt on domestic violence and child protection', Women's Aid, 2004, p. 7.

14 Adapted from *Shattered Love . . . Broken Lives. . .*: A domestic violence resource pack from the Domestic Violence Task Group of Churches Together in the Merseyside Region.

15 *Shattered Love . . . Broken Lives. . .*

16 Taken from the leaflet on domestic violence, 'Violence: financial control, emotional abuse', Home Office, June 2004.

17 Statement on Minimum Standards of Practice by the RESPECT organization, at http://www.changeweb.org.uk.

18 Taken from the leaflet, 'Action on elder abuse for volunteers, paid workers and advocates' published by Action on Elder Abuse (see Resources, Appendix 7). More information on abuse of vulnerable adults is available from the House of Bishops' guidelines on vulnerable adults, *Promoting a safe church*.

19 We are grateful for the help of the Southall Black Sisters in compiling this section and Appendix 10.

20 *Tackling Domestic Abuse: Silence is not always golden*, p. 5. Published by the NUT, www.teachers.org.uk.

21 Adapted from the forthcoming House of Bishops report on vulnerable adults, *Promoting a safe church*.

22 'What to do if you're worried a child is being abused', Department of Health, 2003, Appendix 3, sections 10 and 11.

23 This, and other issues relating to confidentiality, are given detailed consideration by the Legal Advisory Commission in its opinion entitled 'The Clergy and Confidentiality' (May 2002), to be published in the forthcoming edition of *Legal Opinions concerning the Church of England.*

24 Data Protection (Processing Sensitive Personal Data) Order 2000. Schedule para. 4.

25 Data Protection Act 1998 s29(1).

26 The judgement of the House of Lords in *Parochial Church Council of Aston Cantlow and Wilmcote with Billesley, Warwickshire v Wallbank and another* delivered on 26 June 2003.

27 The Southall Black Sisters have helped us compile this appendix.

28 In addition, the Southall Black Sisters argue that the multicultural approach assumes that minority communities are homogeneous entities and does not acknowledge the internal differences which give rise to power and privilege imbalance and lead to marginalized people being ignored or considered 'inauthentic'. They maintain that non-intervention results in the application of a different standard of rights to women and children and renders them more vulnerable. A more mature multiculturalism demands that all forms of abuse are treated as such irrespective of the context in which it occurs and should be embedded in the service delivery of all voluntary and statutory agencies.

29 For a further article on this see James Woodward's 'The not-so-good life? Living and learning alongside older people', published on the Leveson Centre web site, http://www.levesoncentre.org.uk. James Woodward is director of the Centre.

30 In form 2 of the Common Worship service, the bridegroom may say 'to love and to cherish', whereas the woman can say 'to love, cherish and obey'.

31 *Domestic Abuse and the Methodist Church: Taking Action*, Methodist Publishing House, 2005.

32 For example Andrew Body, *Growing Together: a guide for couples getting married*, Church House Publishing, 2005. This has useful stories and questions for couples to discuss.

33 Obviously a domestic abuse leaflet should be available.

34 See *Circles of Support and Accountability in the Thames Valley: the first three years, April 2002 to March 2005*, Quaker Communications for Quaker Peace and Social Witness, 2005.

35 *Meeting the Challenge: How the Churches Should Respond to Sex Offenders*, Church of England Board for Social Responsibility, 1999.

36 The bishop has the power to do this automatically, outside the normal complaint procedure but must consult the President of Tribunals first. If a priest who has committed an act of abuse is convicted but avoids a prison sentence, then a penalty could only be imposed if a formal complaint were made under the CDM. See http://www.cofe.anglican.org.

37 Under Canon E 6.